# MAKE 24 PAPER PLANES

Planes: Kees Moerbeek
Text: Elizabeth Golding
Design: Anton Poitier & Ben Potter

## Contents

**B.E.S.**
PUBLISHING

# Let's get started

This book includes simple step-by-step picture instructions to make 24 paper planes, all included with the book. Each plane is marked with fold lines to show you where to crease and fold the paper. There are also elastic bands to attach to the planes and a launcher. Assemble the launcher, then you'll be ready to fly your planes as you build them.

## Attach the elastic band

When you have folded each plane, you will find a mark in the bottom of the fuselage for an elastic band. Make a hole at this mark with a paper punch.

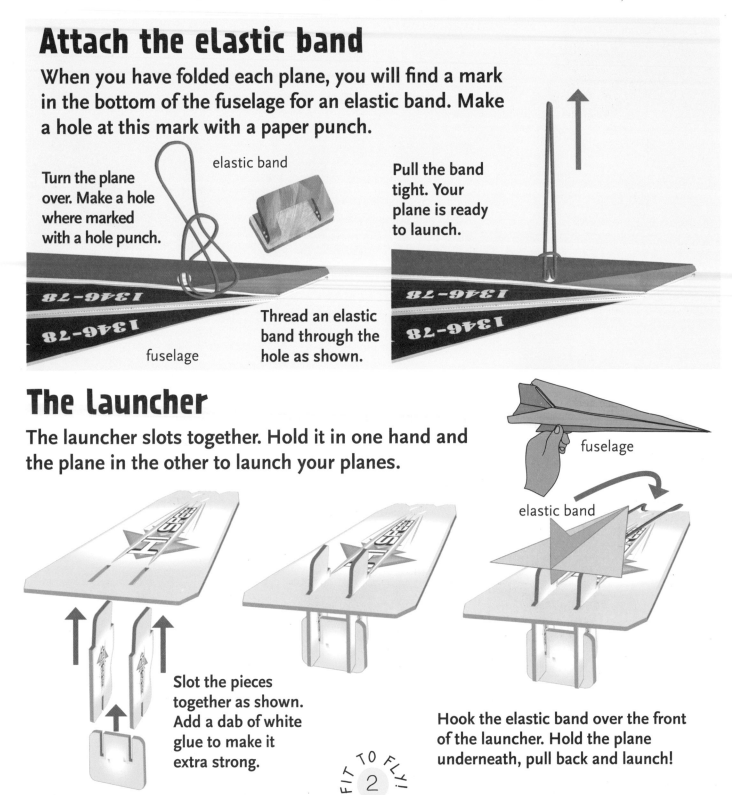

elastic band

Turn the plane over. Make a hole where marked with a hole punch.

Pull the band tight. Your plane is ready to launch.

Thread an elastic band through the hole as shown.

fuselage

1346-78

## The launcher

The launcher slots together. Hold it in one hand and the plane in the other to launch your planes.

fuselage

elastic band

Slot the pieces together as shown. Add a dab of white glue to make it extra strong.

Hook the elastic band over the front of the launcher. Hold the plane underneath, pull back and launch!

# Build a fleet of planes

Build all these planes to make your own flying fleet! Experiment to get the best performance from each plane. There are hints and tips with the instructions. Use the stickers in the pack to decorate each plane as you like.

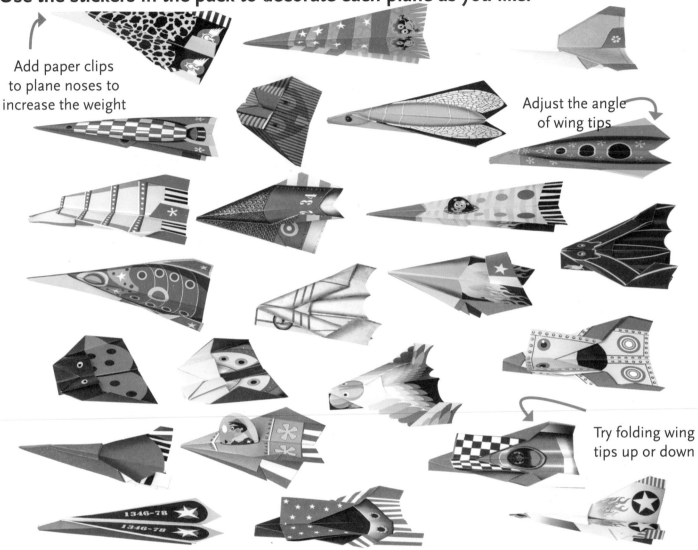

Add paper clips to plane noses to increase the weight

Adjust the angle of wing tips

Try folding wing tips up or down

# Be a safe pilot!

Your planes will fly fast when you launch them! To get your pilot's license, you must follow these simple rules:

1. Don't point your planes at people or animals.

2. Find a safe place to fly, with a clear space and no obstructions.

3. Never fly your planes outside near traffic.

# Hot rod

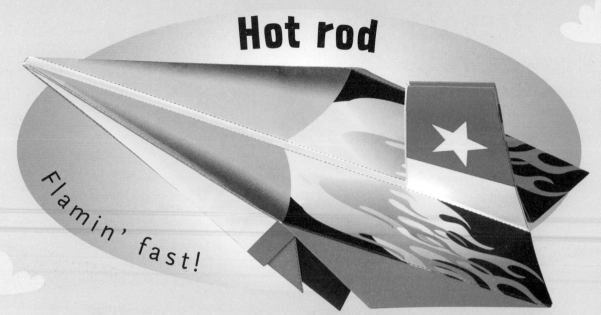

*Flamin' fast!*

Hot rod flies in a curve. Experiment by folding the wing tips up or down to see how this affects the flight path. You should be able to get the plane to fly upward, then dip down to a gentle glide by varying the amount of power.

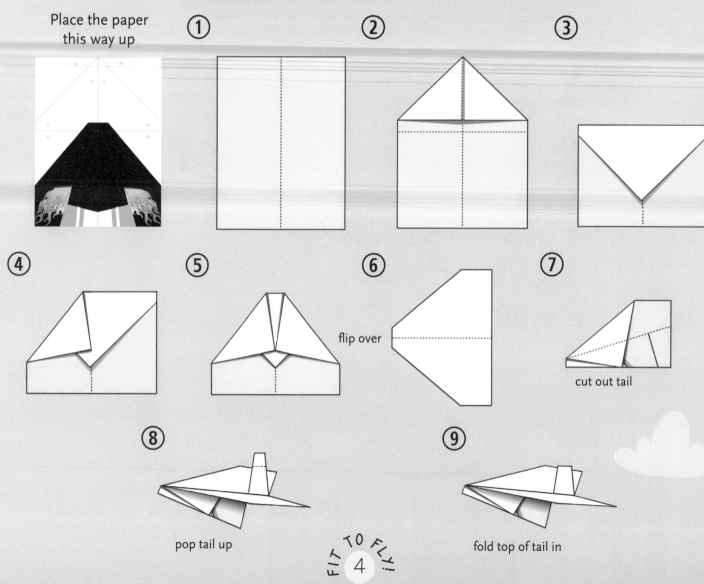

Place the paper this way up

① ② ③

④ ⑤ ⑥ flip over ⑦ cut out tail

⑧ pop tail up ⑨ fold top of tail in

# Zoomer

Woah!

Zoomer flies high and fast, and it goes in a curve. Experiment with the wing flaps by moving them up or down to see how you can affect the performance.

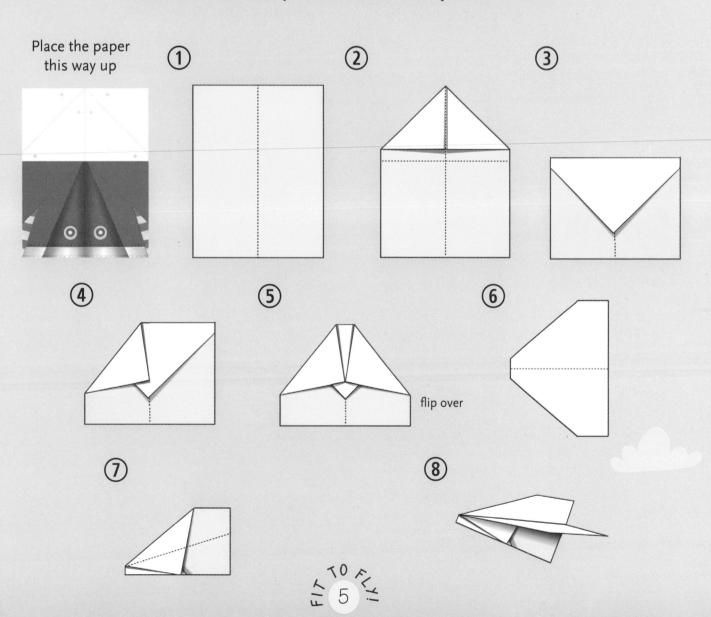

Place the paper this way up

① ② ③

④ ⑤ flip over ⑥

⑦ ⑧

# Whizzer

## Up and away!

This funny little plane works well over short distances by flying in an "S"-shaped curve. Experiment a little with the launch power and see what you can do to change the flight path.

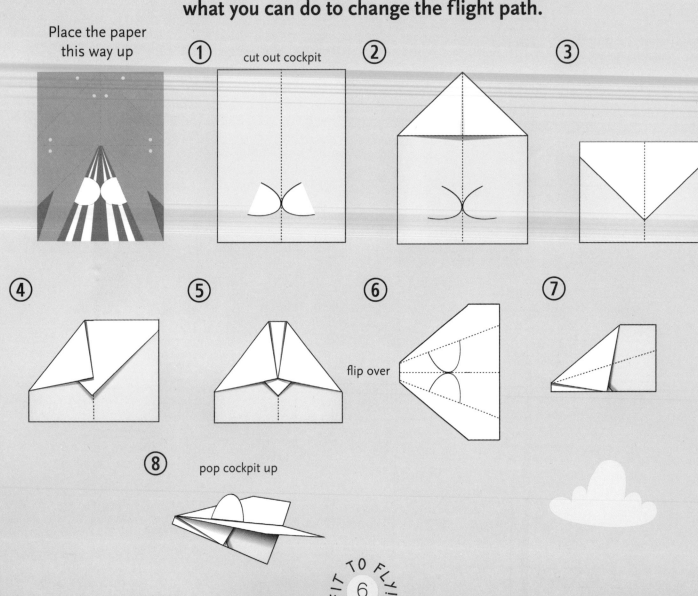

Place the paper this way up

① cut out cockpit

②

③

④

⑤

⑥ flip over

⑦

⑧ pop cockpit up

# The arrow

## Flies straight and true

The Arrow goes fast, and it flies very straight and high if you aim the launcher upward. Pull the plane from the back of the fuselage. Straighten the nose if it gets a little bent after repeated flying — try not to aim at walls or the nose will bend!

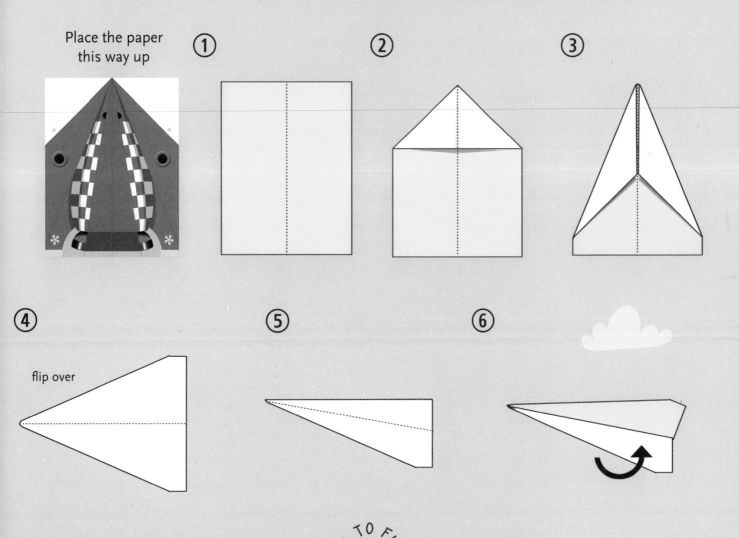

Place the paper this way up

① ② ③

④ flip over ⑤ ⑥

# Classic dart

**Bulls-eye!**

The Dart is a classic design that's really easy to make and fly. For added speed, try attaching a paperclip just under the nose, and just watch it zoom! Don't forget to add some stickers to customize the design to make it your own.

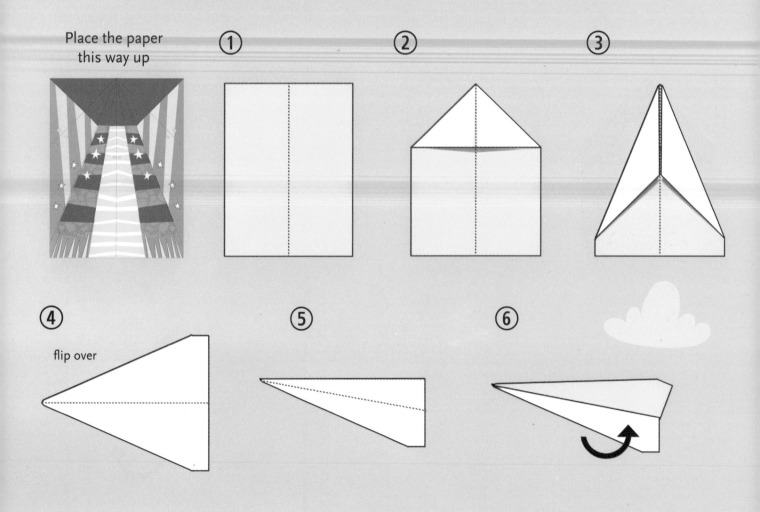

Place the paper this way up

① ② ③

④ flip over

⑤ ⑥

# Alien arrow

## Look who's flying!

The Alien Arrow is a dart design that flies straight and fast. After attaching the elastic band, hold the plane immediately under the pilot or the plane will bend. Don't forget to add some stickers to customize the design to make it your own.

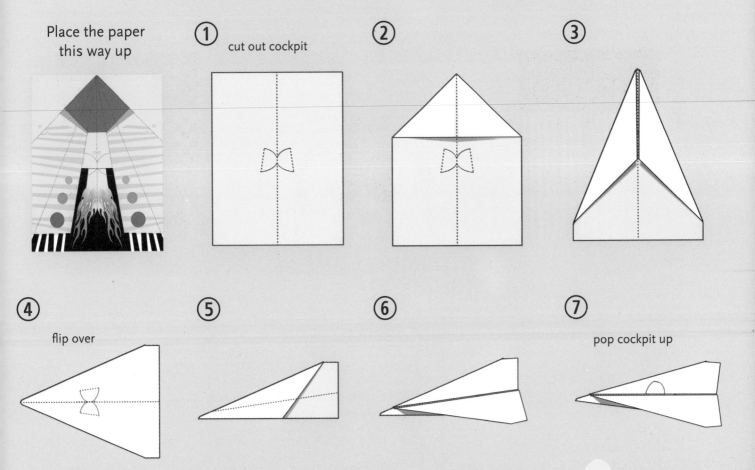

Place the paper this way up

① cut out cockpit

②

③

④ flip over

⑤

⑥

⑦ pop cockpit up

# Flying duck

*Fly me fast!*

The Flying Duck is a strange looking machine, but it twists and turns if you fly it fast. Hold the fuselage well back and pull hard on the elastic band before you let go, and watch it zoom! There are three different designs for this plane, all with the same folds.

Place the paper
this way up

| Flying duck | Spy plane | Flying ace |
|---|---|---|
| 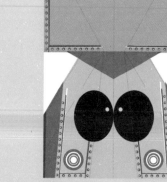 | 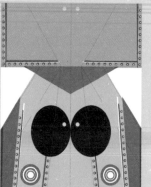 |  |
| ① | ② | ③ |

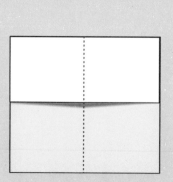

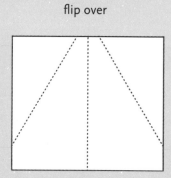

flip over

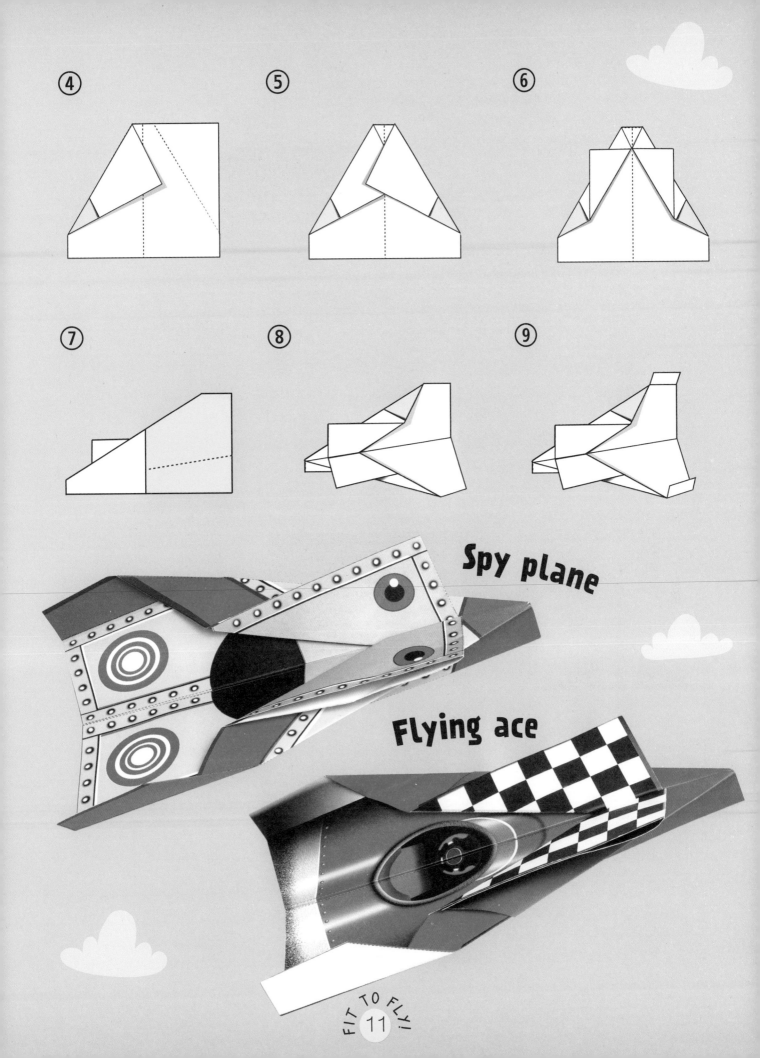

④ ⑤ ⑥

⑦ ⑧ ⑨

**Spy plane**

**Flying ace**

# Condor

*Swoop low!*

The Condor swoops and curves, depending on how hard you pull the elastic band. You might need to practice a little with this bird and add a paperclip to the nose to get good balance. There are three different designs for this plane, all with the same folds.

Place the paper
this way up

| Condor | The bat | Old timer |

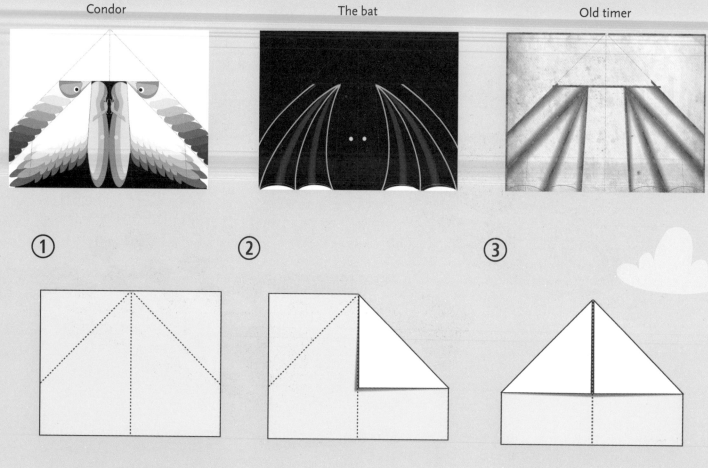

① ② ③

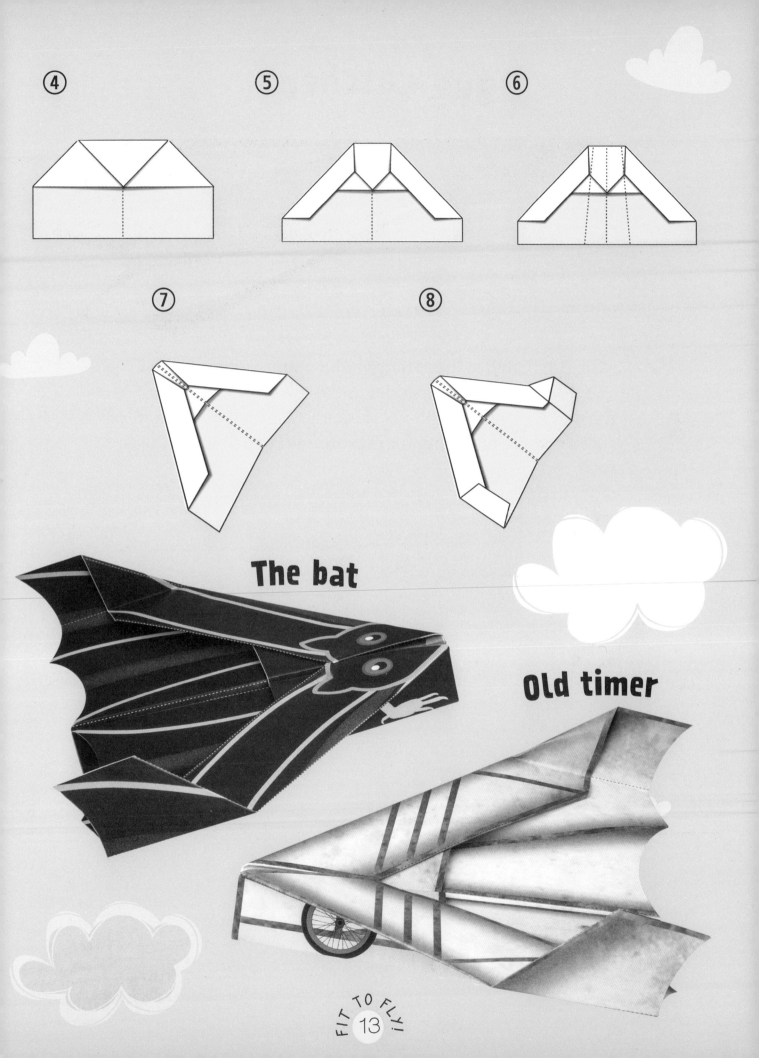

④ ⑤ ⑥

⑦ ⑧

**The bat**

**Old timer**

# Bug catcher

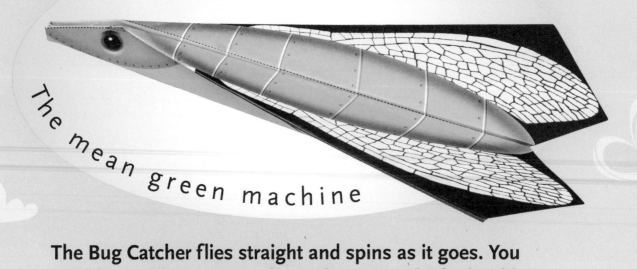

## The mean green machine

**The Bug Catcher flies straight and spins as it goes. You could try adding a paperclip to the nose, which should make it fly straight without spinning. Aim the plane high when launching for maximum flight time.**

Place the paper this way up

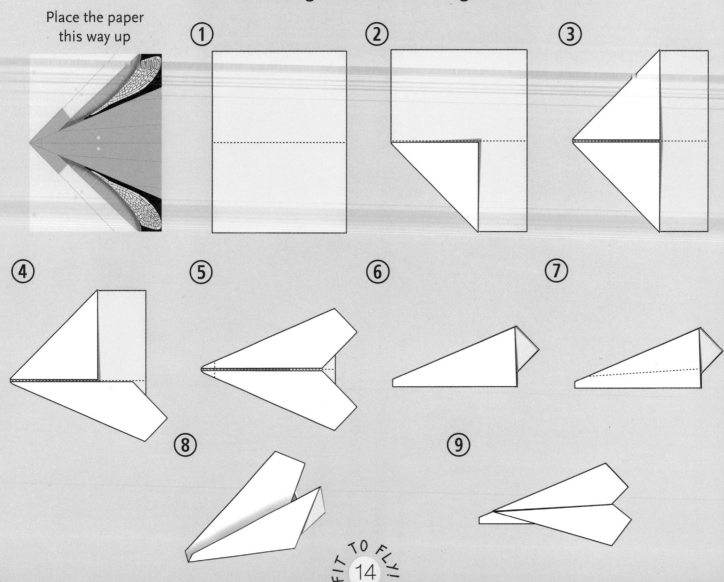

# Delta 1

**1346-78**
**1346-78**

Flies straight and true

Delta 1 is the same basic design as the Bug Catcher. It also flies straight with a bit of a spin. You could experiment by adding a paperclip to the nose to keep the plane straight and level.

Place the paper this way up

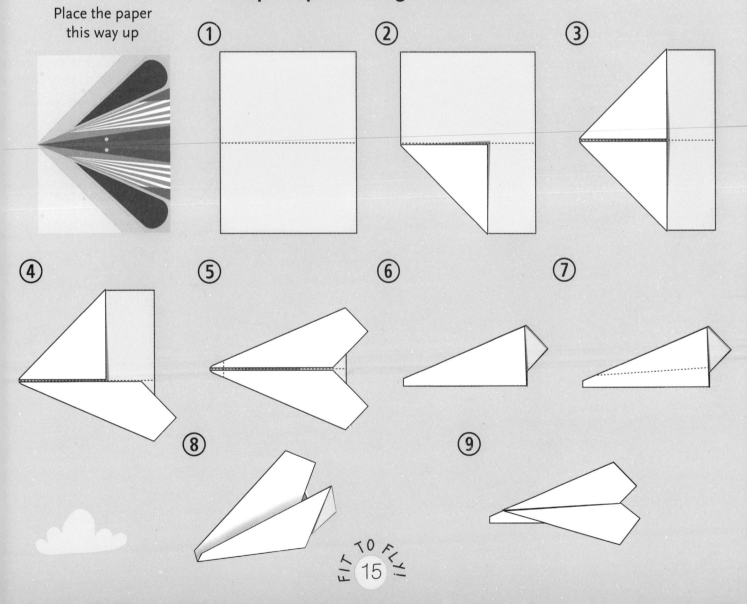

# Delta 2

*Flies well for you!*

Delta 2 spins through the air when launched at speed. It will fly straight and in a nice curve, spinning as it begins to land. Try adjusting the launch power to see if this affects the flight.

Place the paper this way up

① ② ③

④ ⑤ ⑥ ⑦

⑧ ⑨

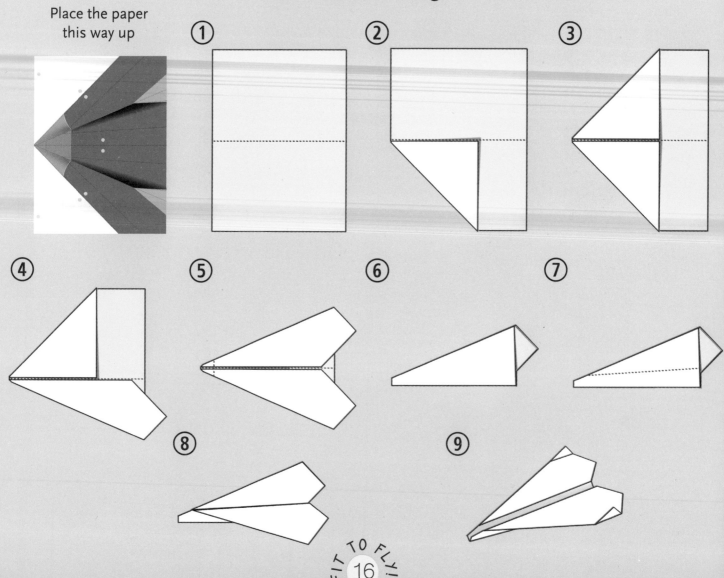

# Interceptor

## Radar detector!

This plane flies straight, with a spin before it lands.
Try to adjust the wing tips and add a paperclip to the nose
to experiment with the Interceptor's flight path.

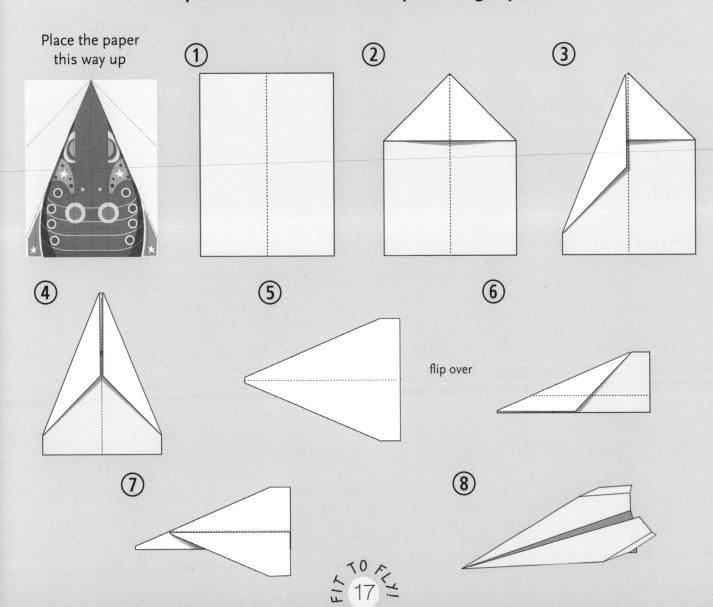

Place the paper
this way up

① ② ③

④ ⑤ ⑥

flip over

⑦ ⑧

# Razor

## Jet-powered!

Razor flies high, but you need to experiment with the amount of power you use. It spins a little before it lands, but should fly in a nice curve.

Place the paper this way up

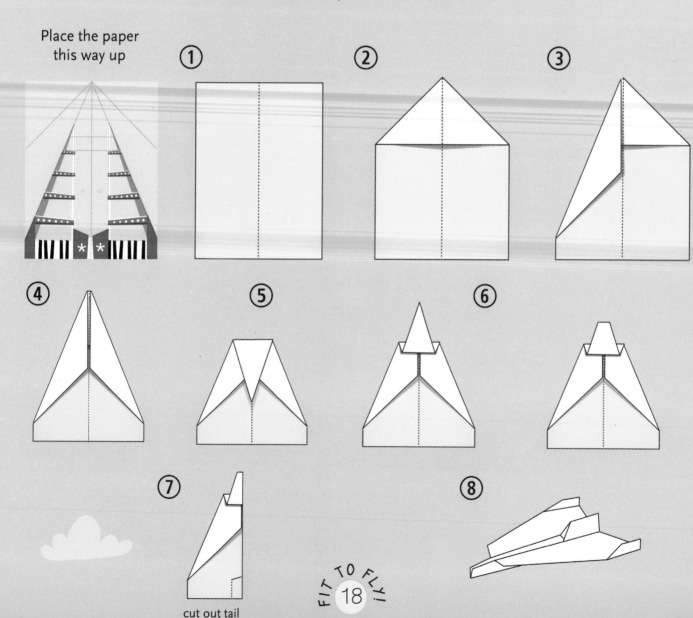

① ② ③

④ ⑤ ⑥

⑦ cut out tail

⑧

# XLR8

*Lift and zoom!*

XLR8 flies straight with a spin. You could experiment with the wing-tip flaps to lift them up or down to see if this changes the flight path. Add a paperclip to the nose, too, to see if this changes the flight.

Place the paper this way up

① ② ③

④ ⑤ ⑥

flip over

⑦ ⑧

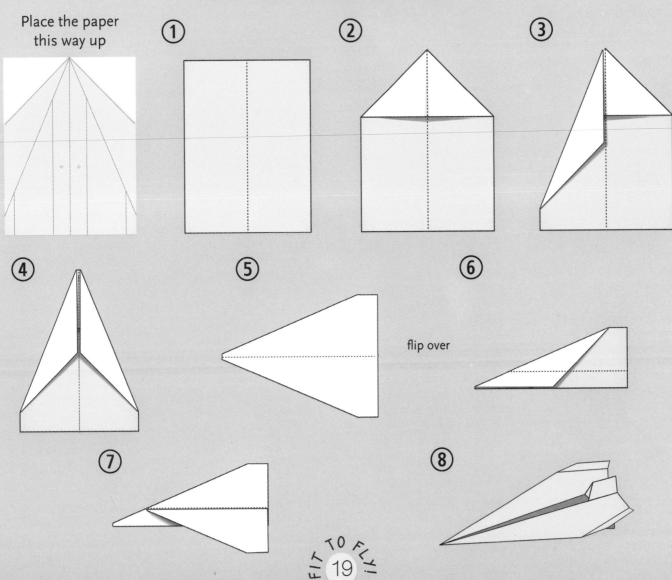

# The Spitfire

## Built for speed!

The Spitfire flies far and fast. There are three different models using the same basic folds. One has a tail fin. You could adjust the wing tips and experiment with this plane. Try bending them up instead of down to see what happens.

Place the paper this way up

| Spitfire | Fire demon | Red Baron |

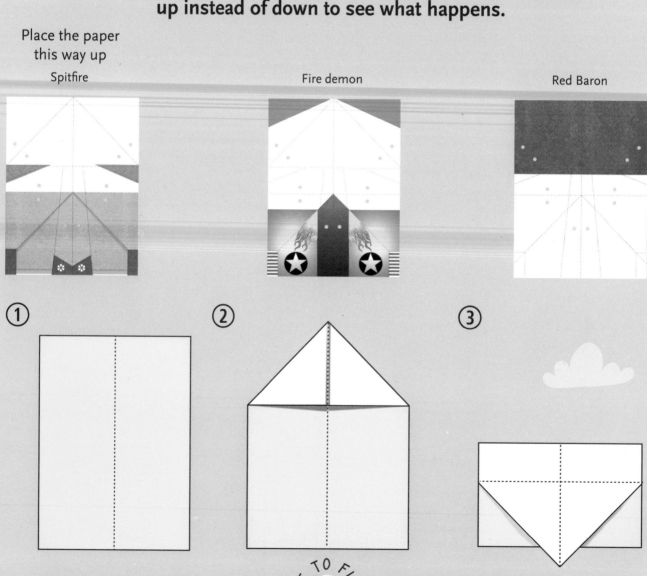

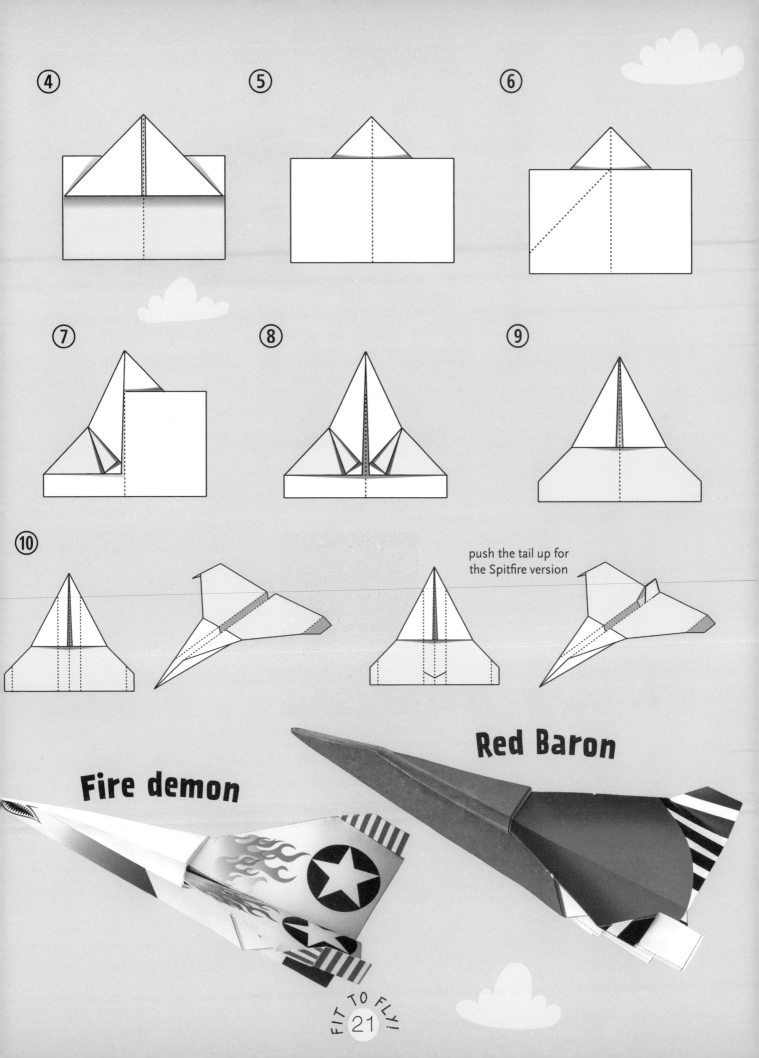

④

⑤

⑥

⑦

⑧

⑨

⑩

push the tail up for
the Spitfire version

**Red Baron**

**Fire demon**

**Glider**

Zzzzz!

The Glider flies very gently if you launch it carefully. Pull lightly on the elastic band launcher to see how it flies, then try again by pulling a little harder. This plane has lots of folds, so take your time. There are three different designs.

Place the paper
this way up

| Glider | Ladybug | Mr. Stripy |
| :---: | :---: | :---: |

① ② ③ ④

⑤

⑥

⑦

⑧

⑨

⑩

A

⑪

B
A

⑫

B

⑬

turn back

⑭

⑮

⑯

# Mr. Stripy

# Ladybug

# Repair workshop

Paper planes tend to get damaged after repeated flights, so here are some simple repair tips. You can also change the performance of your plane by adding a little weight to the nose.

## Stickers

There is a sheet of stickers packed with this book. You can use the stickers to customize any of the planes, but they can also be handy for repairs to small rips and tears. Just place a sticker over the damaged area and carefully press it down to fix the plane.

*ouch!*

## Bent nose

It's easy to bend the end of some of the planes, especially those that have a pointed nose. Straighten out the bend with your fingers, then use a little adhesive tape to strengthen the nose.

## Add weight

You can affect the performance of a plane by adding a little extra weight to its nose. One of the easiest ways of doing this is to use a paper clip, but adhesive putty also does the job. This can also help to fix a damaged nose. WARNING: Do not launch the plane at people or pets, especially if you have weighted the nose!

Push a paper clip over the nose. You can also fix it in place with a little adhesive tape.

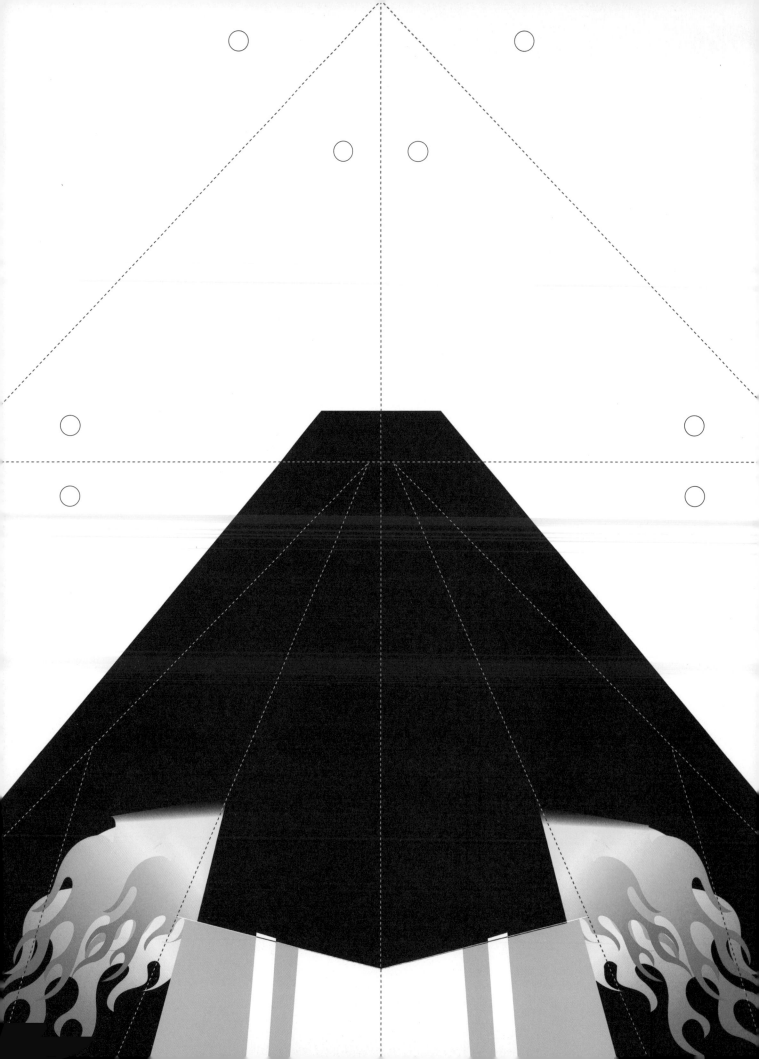

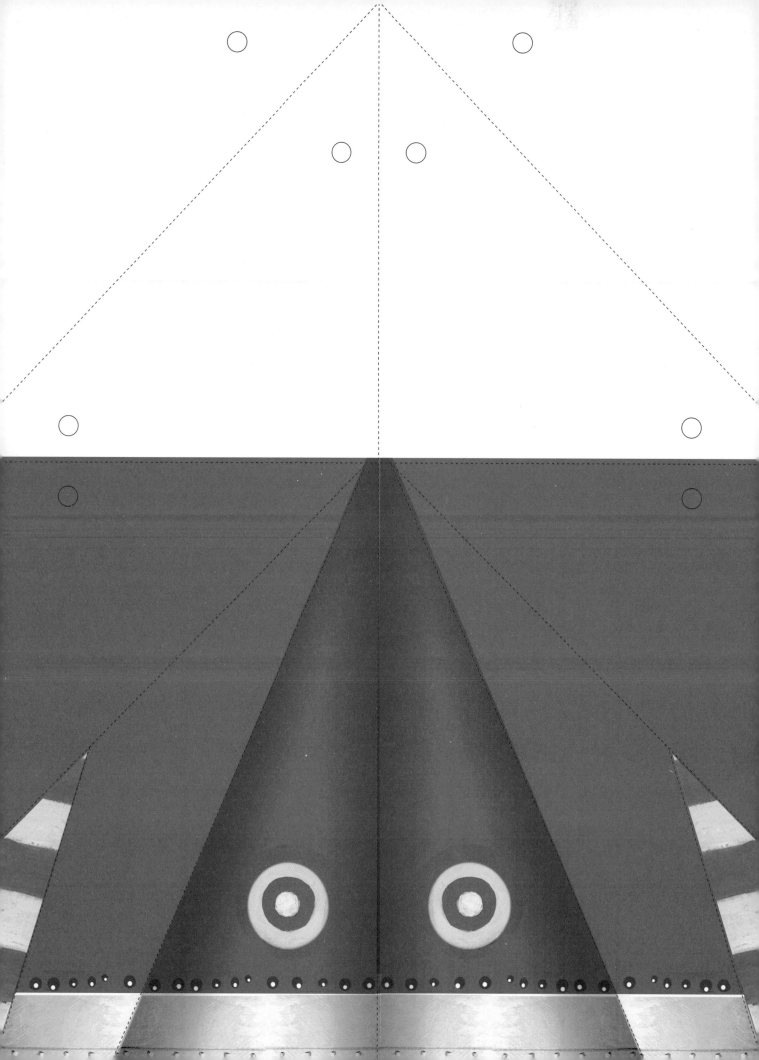

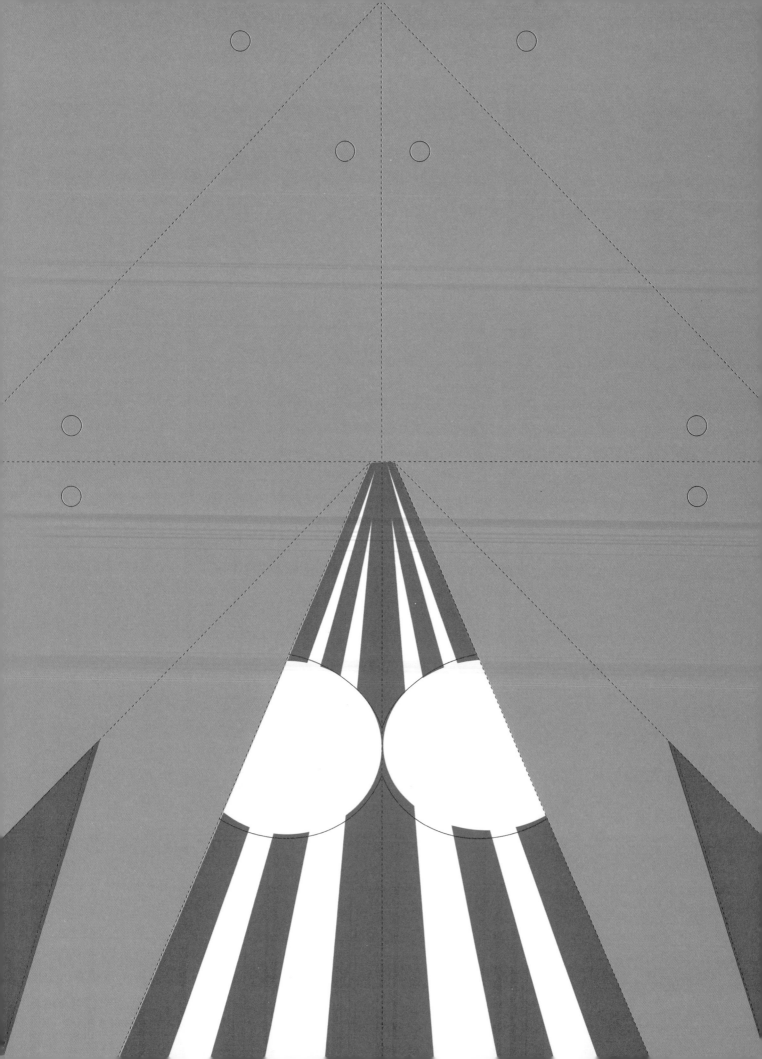

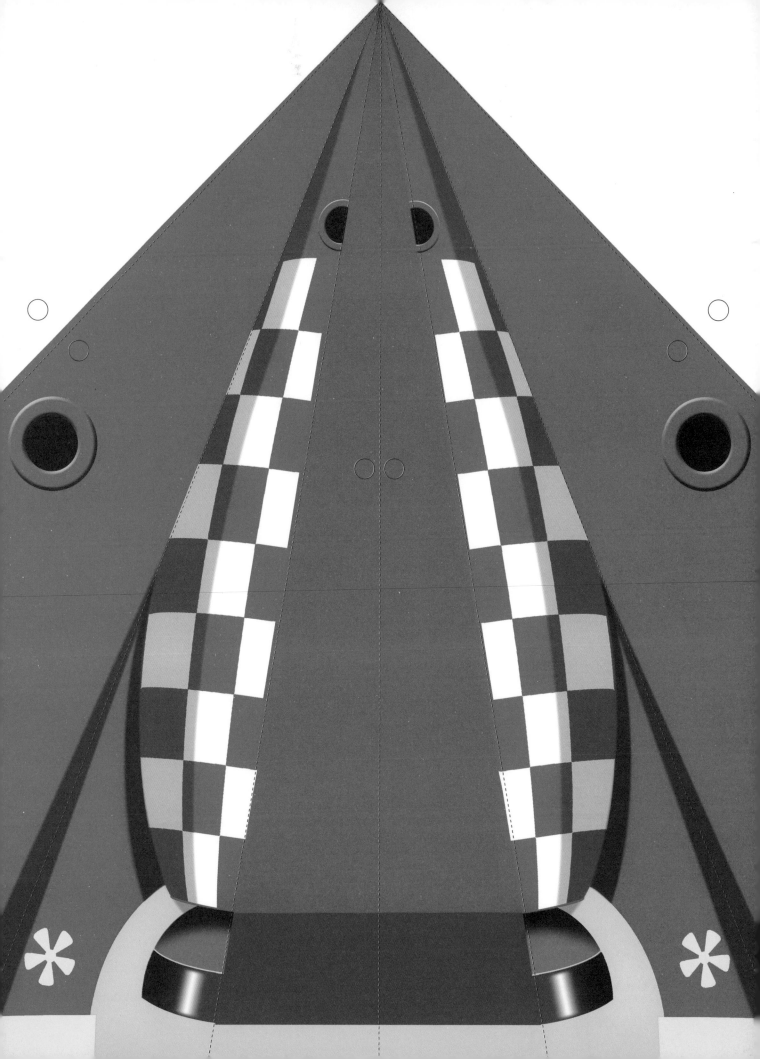

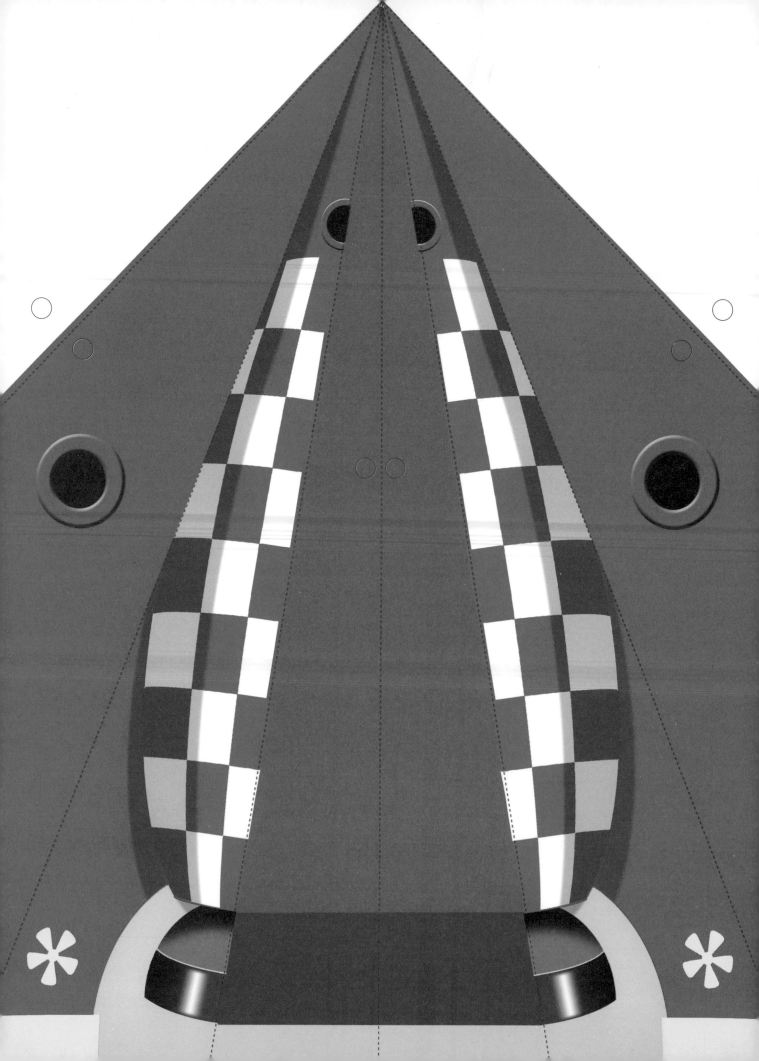

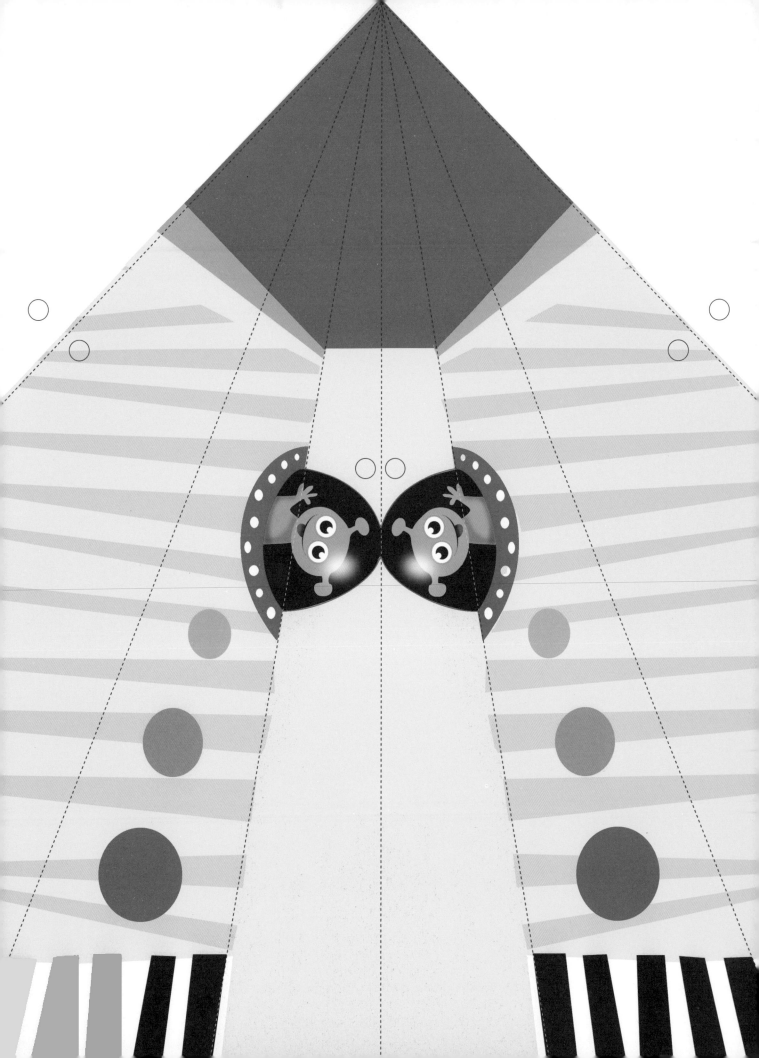

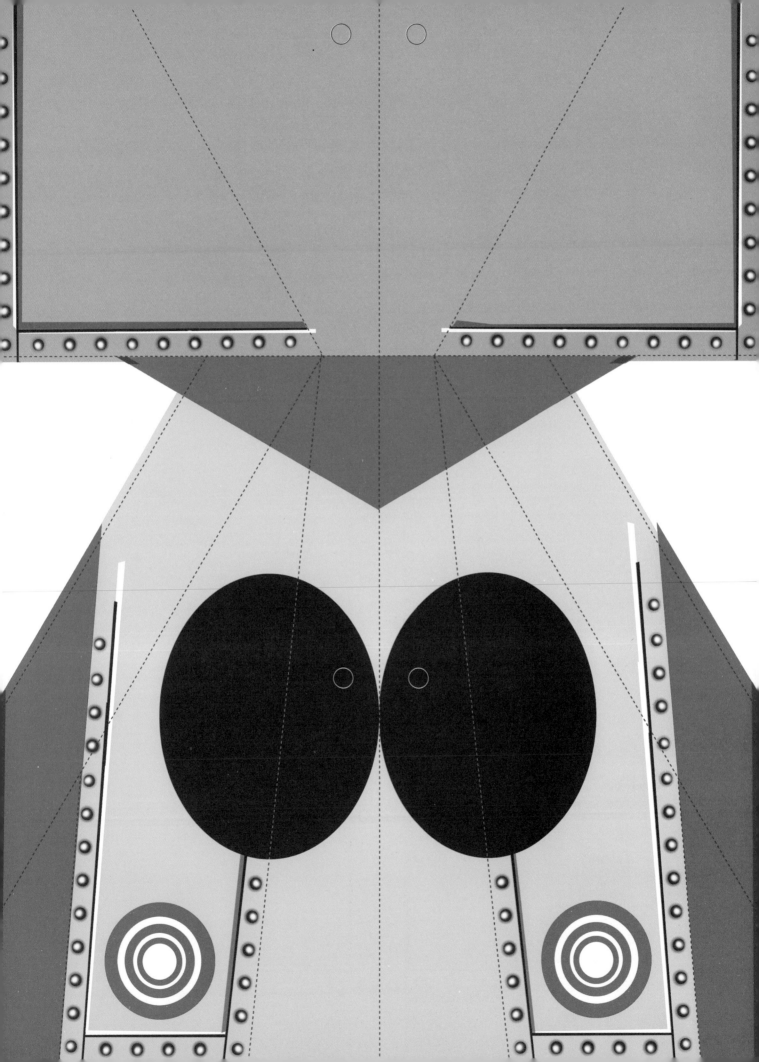

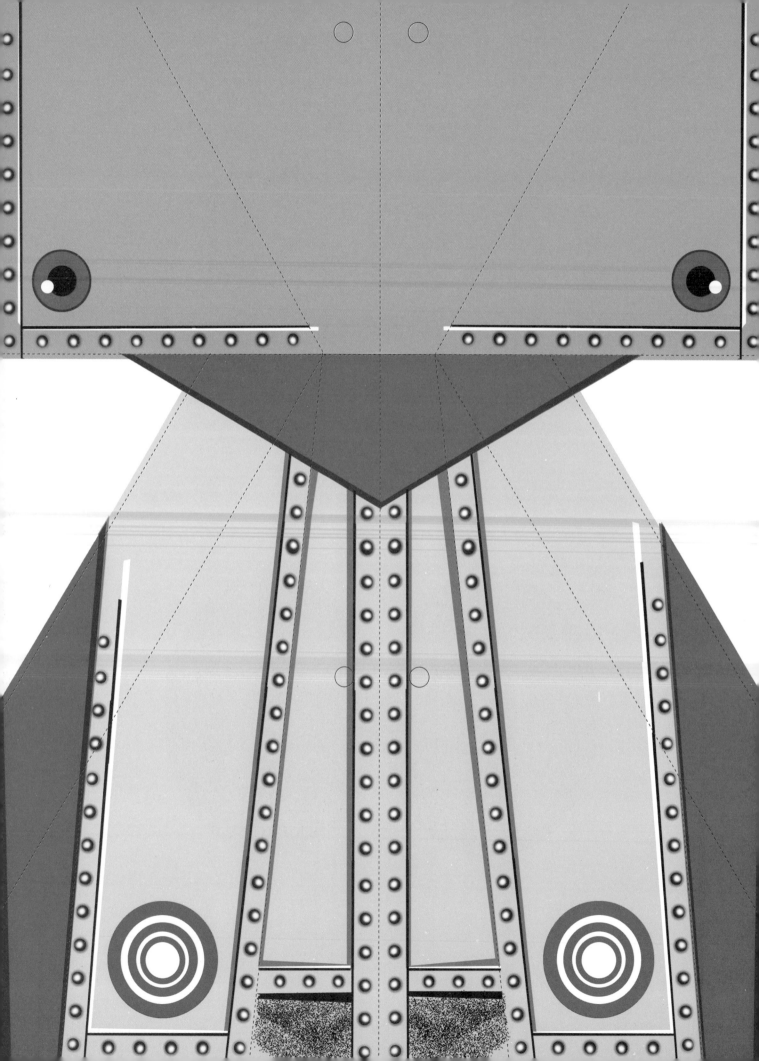

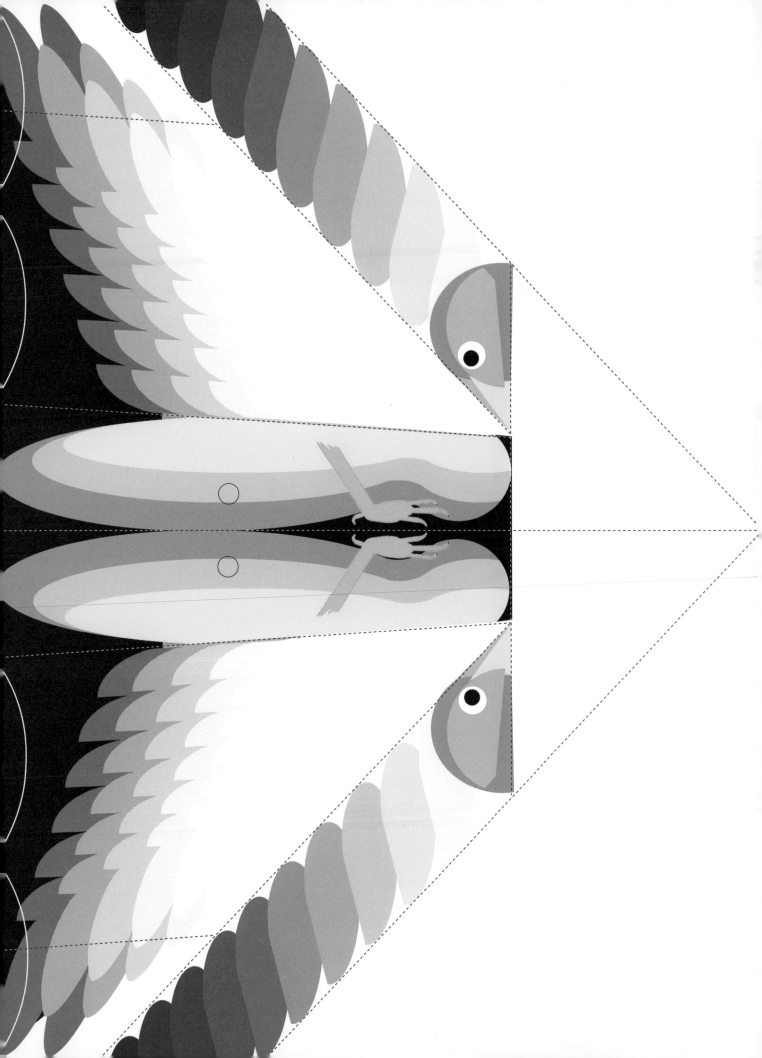

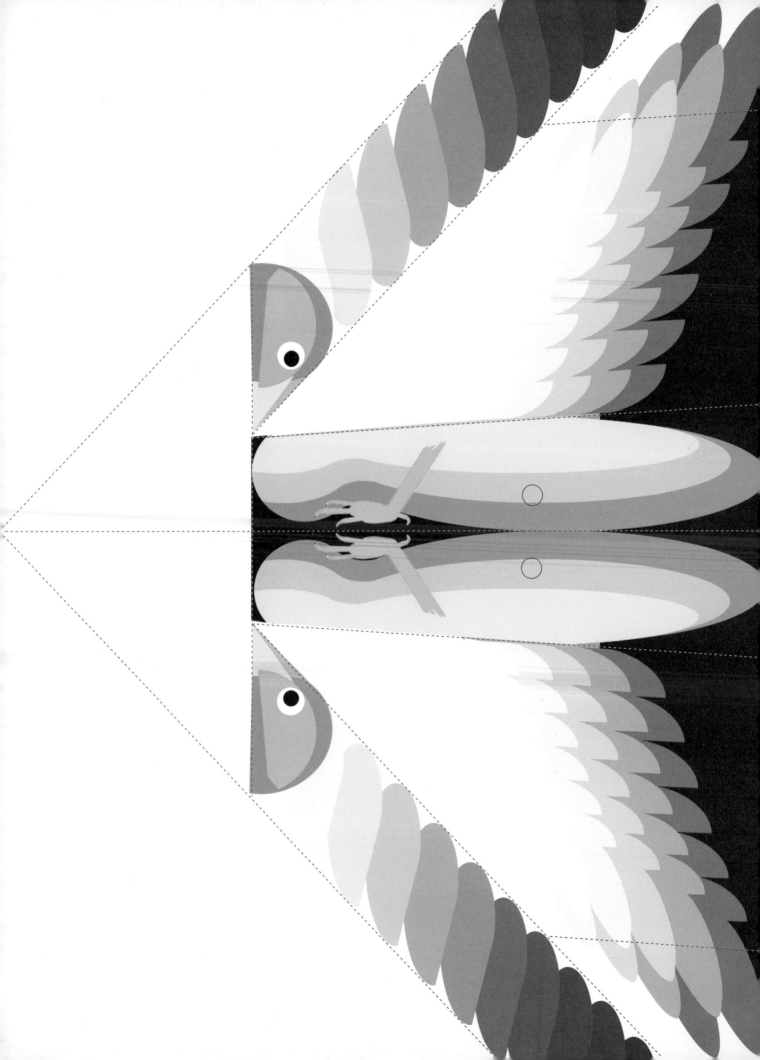

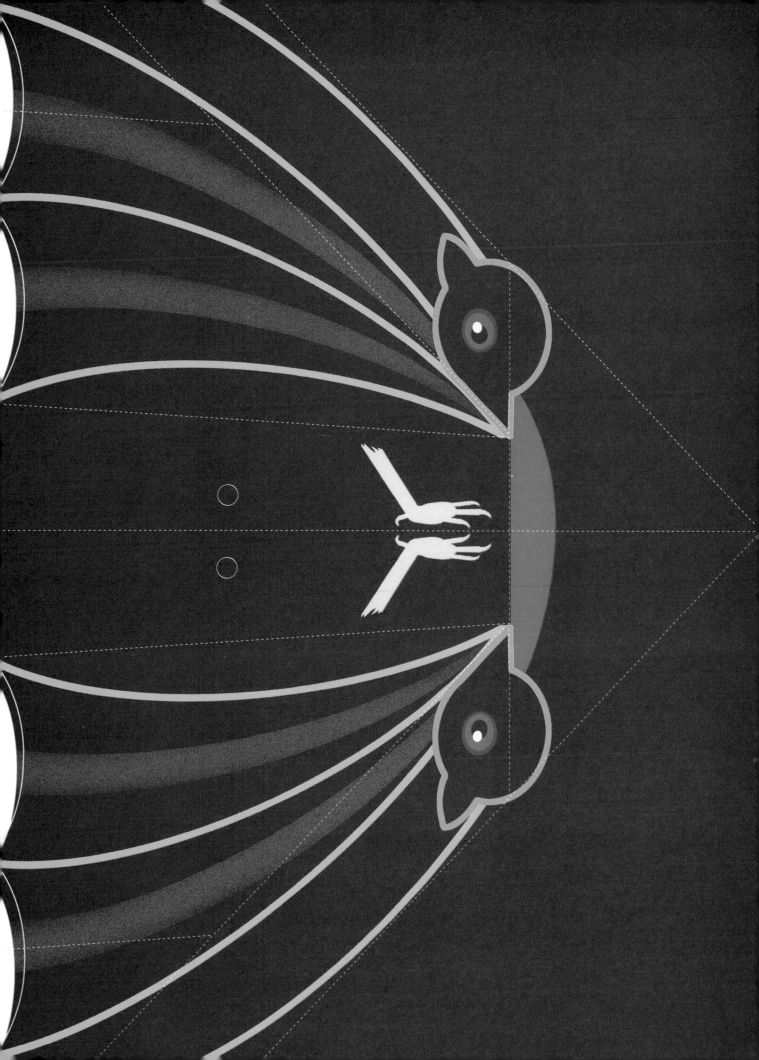

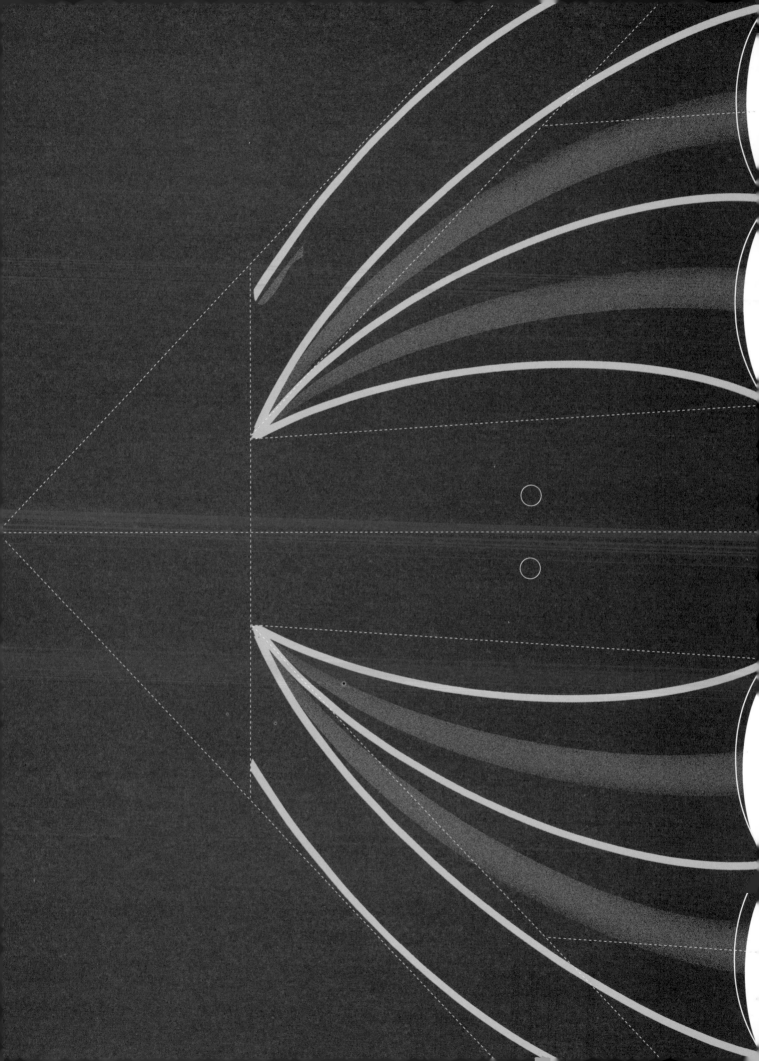

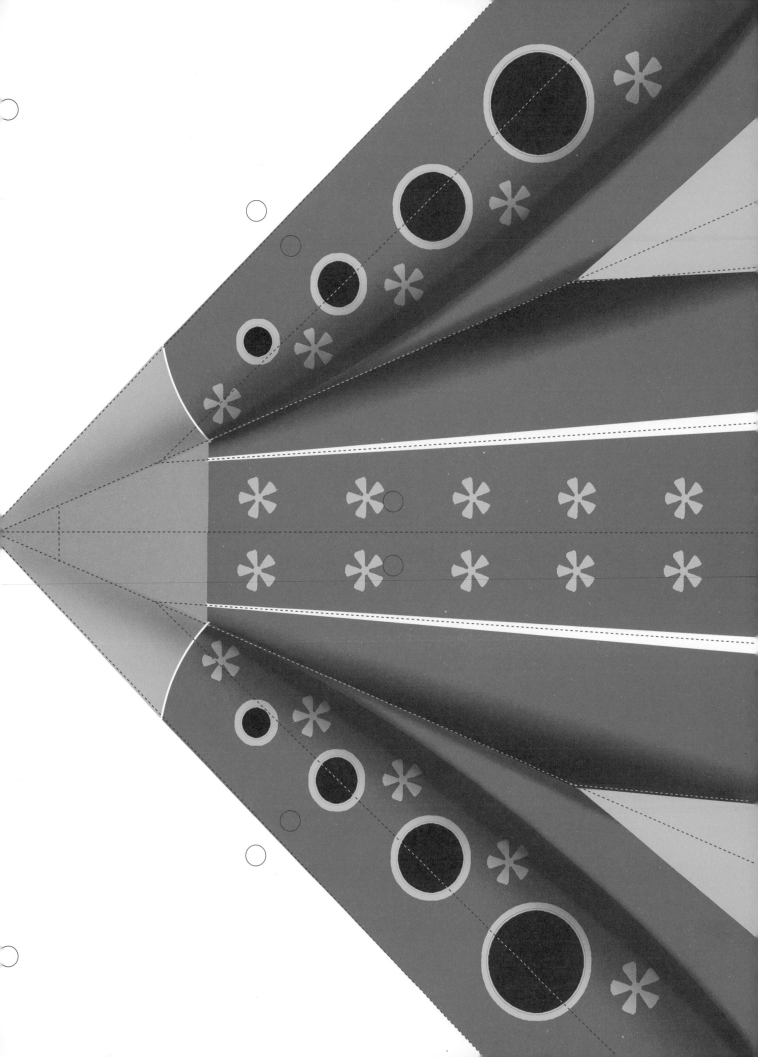

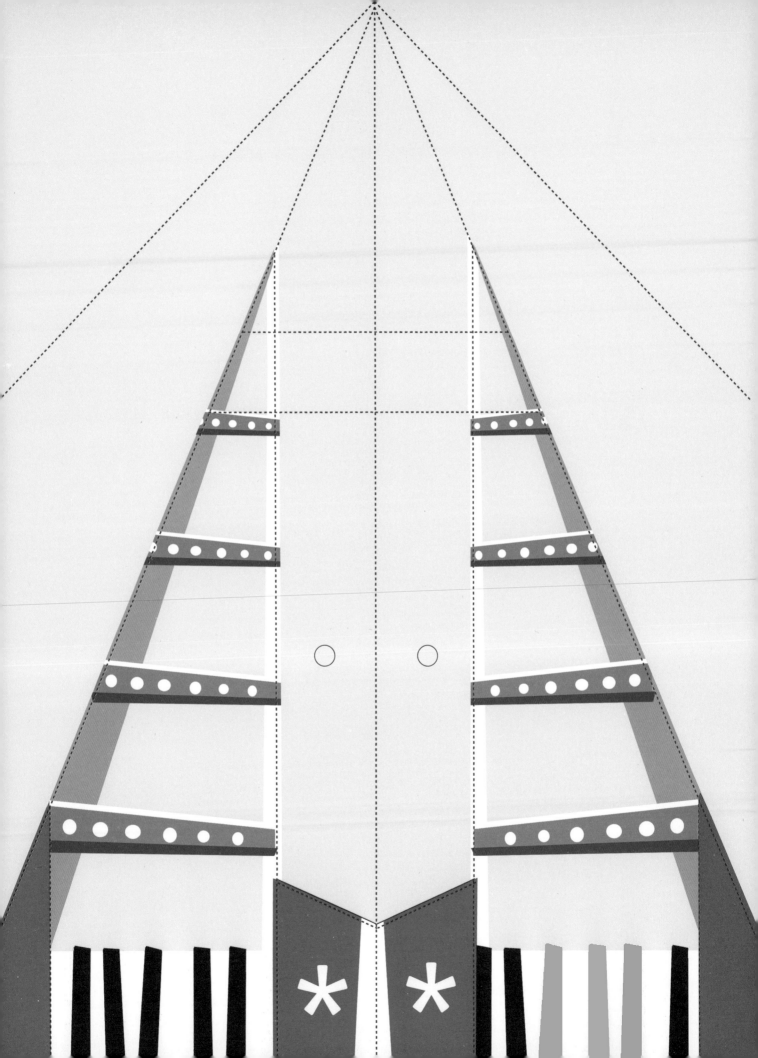

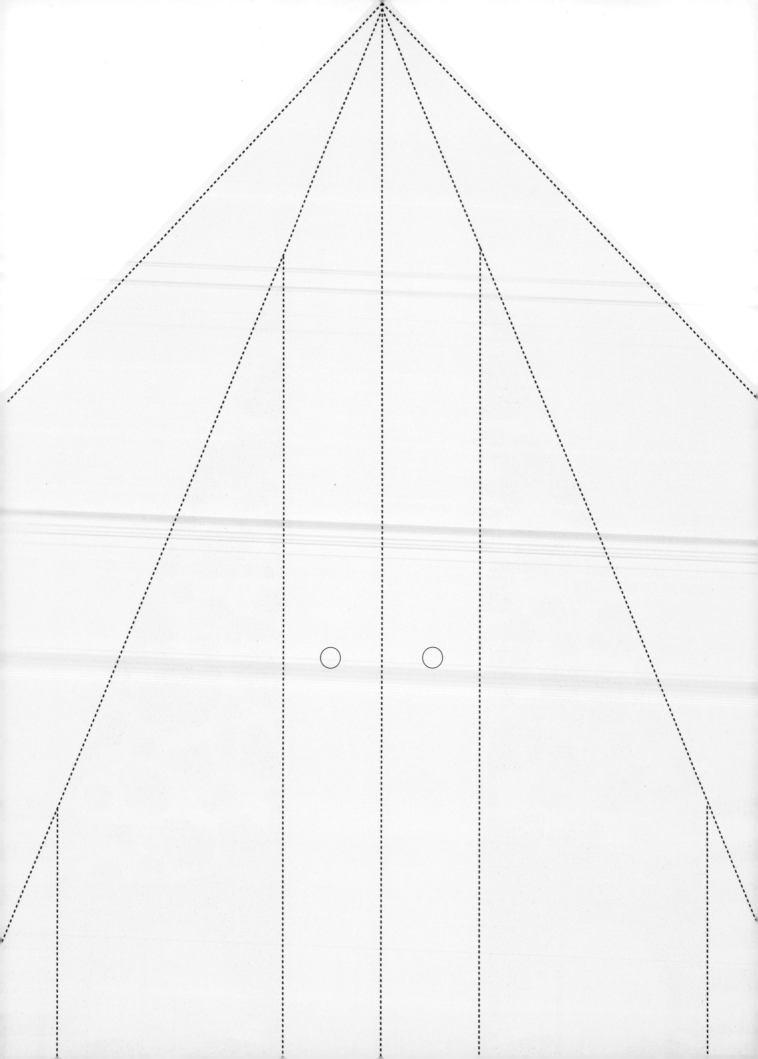

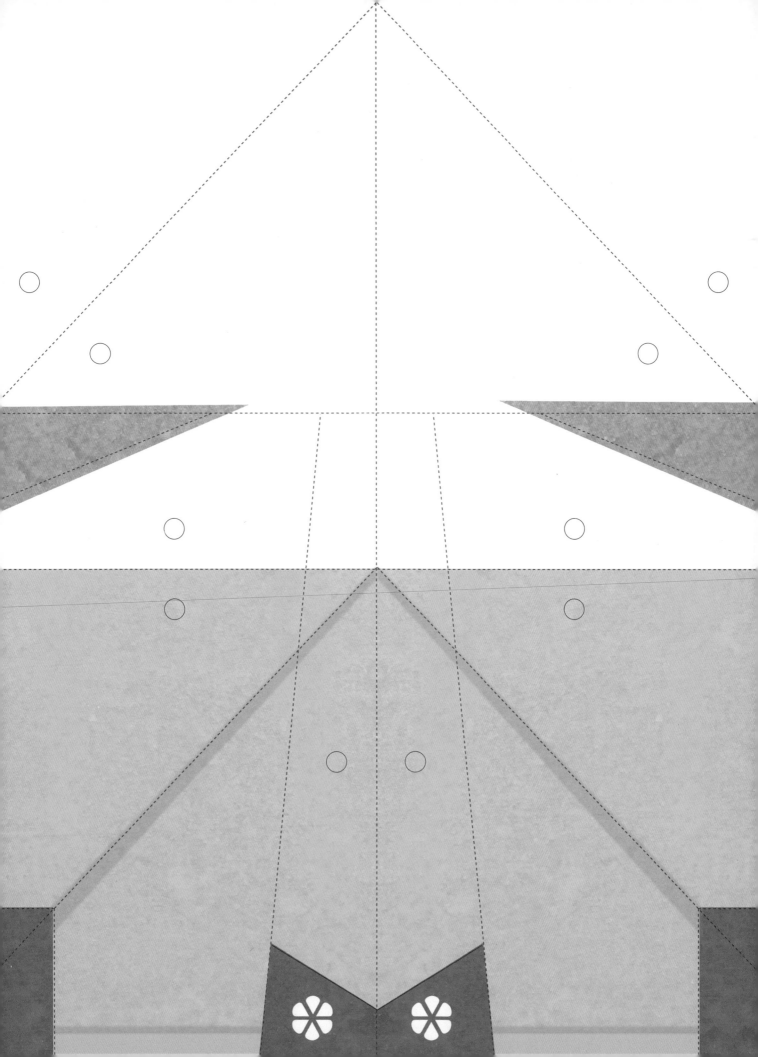

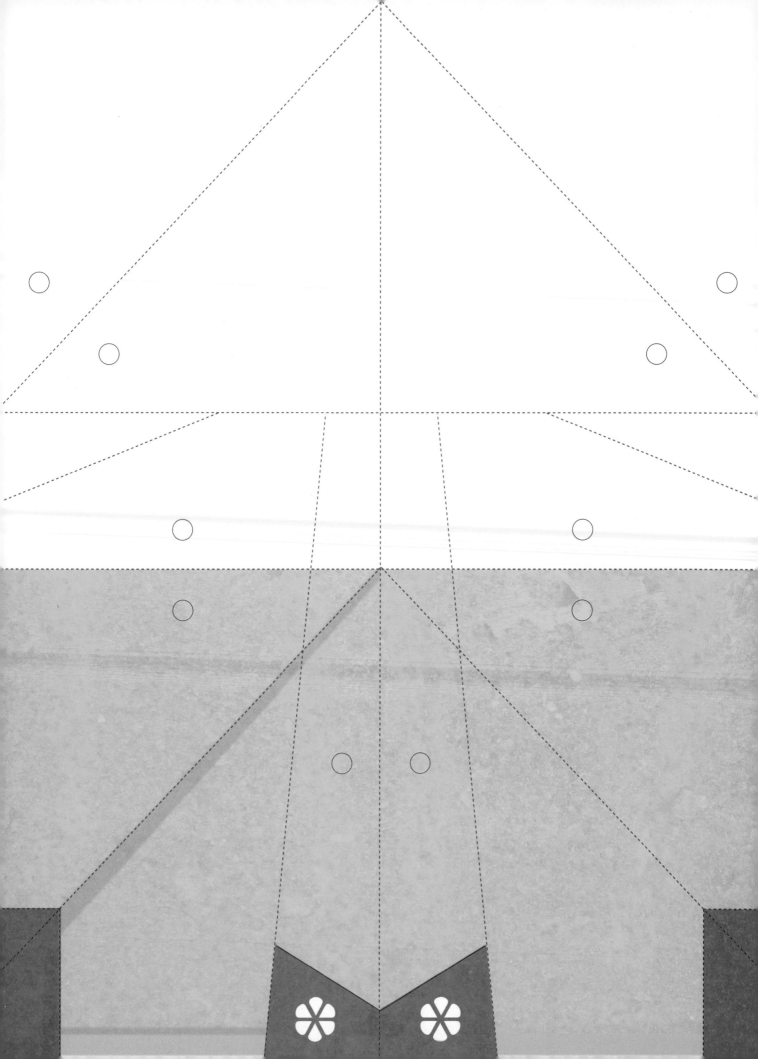

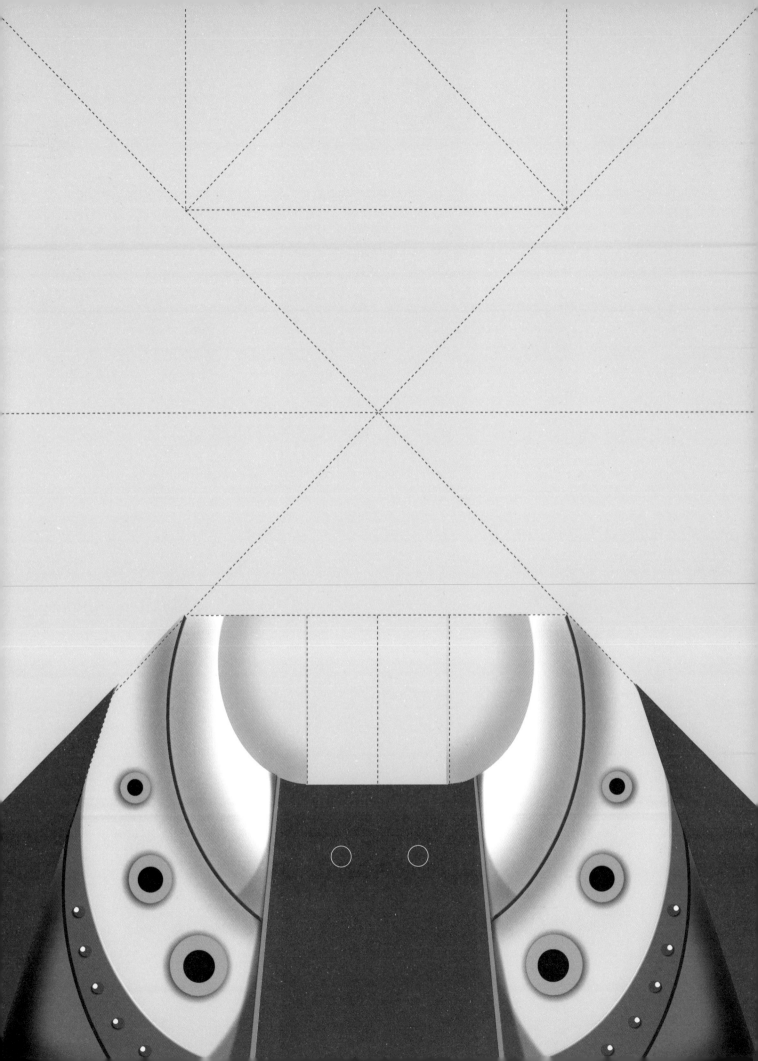

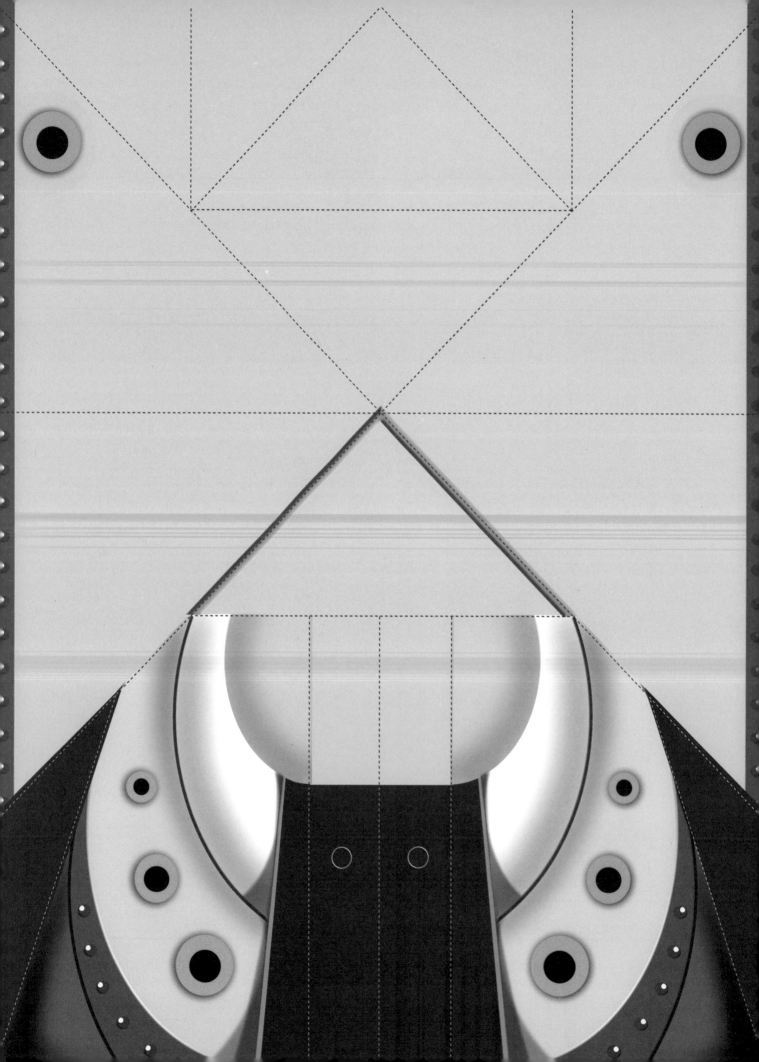

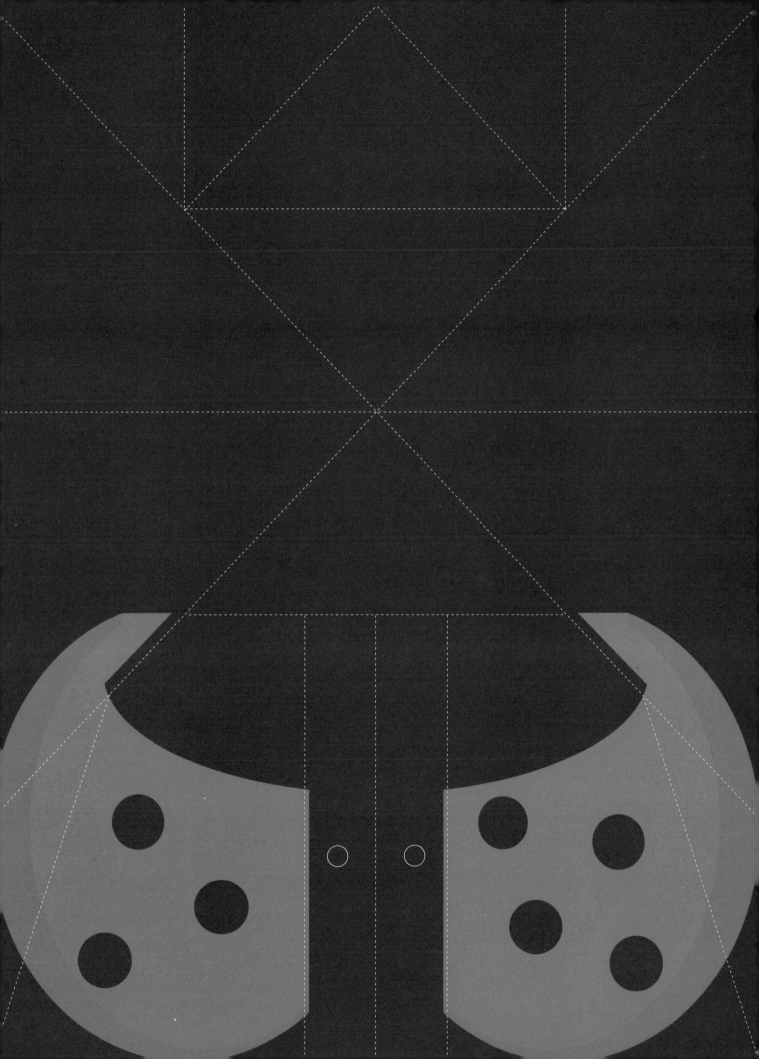

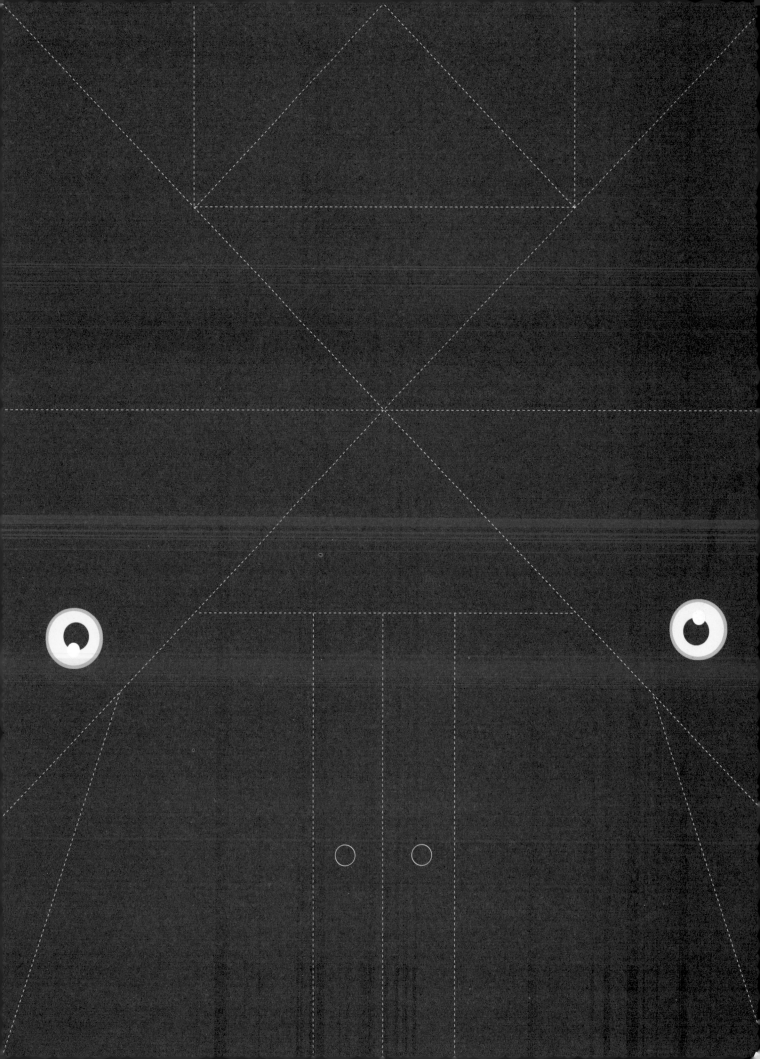